EXPLORING WORLD CULTURES

Greece

Kate Shoup

Cavendish
Square

New York

Published in 2017 by Cavendish Square Publishing, LLC
243 5th Avenue, Suite 136, New York, NY 10016

Library of Congress Cataloging-in-Publication Data

Names: Shoup, Kate, 1972-
Title: Greece / Kate Shoup.
Description: New York : Cavendish Square Publishing, 2017. | Series:
Exploring world cultures | Includes bibliographical references and index.
| Description based on print version record and CIP data provided by publisher; resource not viewed.
Identifiers: LCCN 2015049875 (print) | LCCN 2015048866 (ebook) |
ISBN 9781502617408 (ebook) | ISBN 9781502618139 (paperback) |
ISBN 9781502618054 (library bound) | ISBN 9781502617934 (6 pack)
Subjects: LCSH: Greece--Juvenile literature.
Classification: LCC DF717 (print) | LCC DF717 .S47 2017 (ebook) |
DDC 949.5--dc23
LC record available at http://lccn.loc.gov/2015049875

Editorial Director: David McNamara
Editor: Kristen Susienka
Copy Editor: Rebecca Rohan
Art Director: Jeffrey Talbot
Designer: Joseph Macri
Production Assistant: Karol Szymczuk
Photo Research: J8 Media

Printed in the United States of America

Contents

Introduction 4

Chapter 1   Geography 6

Chapter 2   History 8

Chapter 3   Government 10

Chapter 4   The Economy 12

Chapter 5   The Environment 14

Chapter 6   The People Today 16

Chapter 7   Lifestyle 18

Chapter 8   Religion 20

Chapter 9   Language 22

Chapter 10   Arts and Festivals 24

Chapter 11   Fun and Play 26

Chapter 12   Food 28

Glossary 30

Find Out More 31

Index & About the Author 32

Introduction

Greece is a very old country. It started in 3200 BCE. Many buildings and statues from ancient Greece still stand today.

Much of Greece is covered in mountains. Greece is surrounded by water on three sides. There are many Greek islands. Most of these islands are empty.

People who live in Greece are called Greeks. They speak a language called Greek. Nearly all Greeks are Christian. They belong to the Greek Orthodox Church. About two-thirds of Greeks live in cities, such as Athens. The rest of the people live in rural areas or on islands.

Greece is often called the "cradle of Western civilization." It is an interesting country to learn about.

A view of Athens, the capital of Greece.

Greece is a country in southern Europe. It covers a lot of land—50,949 square miles (131,957 square kilometers).

The main part of Greece is a **peninsula**. It is surrounded by water on three sides. The Aegean Sea is to the east of mainland Greece. The Ionian Sea is to the west. The Mediterranean Sea is to the south. Greece

There are many islands in Greece.

also has more than 1,200 islands. The biggest island in Greece is Crete.

Lonely Islands

Most Greek islands are uninhabited. This means no one lives on them. Only 227 of Greece's islands have people living on them.

There are several mountains in Greece. Many mountains there are covered with forests. Brown bears, deer, lynx, and wild goats live in these forests.

Summers in Greece are hot and dry. Winters are chilly and wet. In the mountains, it snows.

FACT!

The tallest mountain in Greece is Mount Olympus. It is 9,570 feet (2,917 meters) tall.

Mt. Olympus

Greece was one of the world's first countries. It was first called Hellas.

Around 3200 BCE, the first Greek civilization began. Early Greeks lived on islands in the Aegean Sea. Around 1900 BCE, some Greek people moved to the mainland.

FACT!

The Greek classical period was from 500 BCE until 323 BCE. During this time, Greeks developed new ideas in science, mathematics, philosophy, and the arts.

By 750 BCE, Greece was divided into several **city-states**. One was called Athens. Another was called Sparta. These city-states often fought wars against each other. One was the Peloponnesian War. It was fought by Athens and Sparta. Sparta won.

In 146 BCE, the Romans took over Greece. Then came the Byzantines, Serbs, and Ottoman Turks. Greece won its independence in 1832.

An ancient Greek vase

Alexander the Great

Alexander the Great ruled Greece from 336 to 323 BCE. He joined the city-states into a single empire. This empire stretched all the way to India.

Alexander the Great

VOTE ✓

When Greece won its independence, it became a kingdom. Today, it is a **republic**. Its official name is the Hellenic Republic.

Greece's government has three parts:

1. Legislative: This part of the government is called Parliament. It writes new laws.

2. Judicial: This part of the government is made up of the courts.

3. Executive: The president and prime minister make up this part of the government. The president is the head of the republic. The prime minister is in charge of the government.

Parliament

The Greek Parliament has three hundred members. They meet in Athens.

Greece has a document called the constitution that lists the country's basic laws. The first Greek constitution was

The Greek Parliament in Athens

written in 1822. It has been changed several times since then. All Greek citizens eighteen years and older can vote in Greece's elections.

FACT!

The Greeks invented **democracy**. They called it *demokratia*. This meant "rule by the people." The first Greek democracy was in Athens in 507 BCE.

11

Many people in Greece have good jobs. They enjoy life and live comfortably.

Greece's Piraeus port.

Greece's most important industry is shipping. Boats from all over the world carry items to seaside cities in Greece. Greece's fleet of merchant ships is the largest in the world. Many Greeks work in shipping.

Another important industry is tourism. Many tourists visit Greece each year to see its historic sites, like the Acropolis and the Parthenon. Tourists stay in hotels and eat in restaurants. This brings a lot of money into the country.

Tourism

In 2014, more than 23 million people visited Greece. This was a Greek record!

Tourists at the Parthenon.

Some Greeks are farmers. They grow pistachios, rice, olives, figs, tomatoes, almonds, and other crops. Others are fishermen. They fish for sardines and anchovies. Recently, fishing has become more difficult because there are fewer fish in the water than there used to be.

FACT!

Greek money used to be called drachmas. In 2002, drachmas were replaced by euros.

A thick layer of smog covers the city of Athens.

People need clean air and clean water to live. In Greece, some of the air and water is dirty. Trash is also a problem.

In the 1970s, Greece built many new factories. The factories dumped chemicals into rivers and lakes. This polluted the water. The smoke from factories polluted the air. Cars and

To clean up its air, the city of Athens banned private cars from its main streets. It also decreased the number of taxis allowed on the roads.

power plants burned materials that also polluted the air. In Greece's big cities, such as Athens, the air became very dirty.

In the past, Greece buried all its garbage in landfills. Now, these landfills are nearly full. This is a big problem.

A Greek landfill.

FACT!

Greece is cleaning up its air and water. To do this, it uses more and more renewable energy, such as solar power. Also, more Greeks have begun to recycle their garbage.

More than 11 million people live in Greece. Almost two-thirds of them live in cities. The largest city in Greece is Athens. About 4 million people live there.

FACT!

Lately, more people have died in Greece than have been born there. Also, more people have moved *from* Greece than have moved *to* Greece. That means the country's population is shrinking.

Most people who live in Greece come from the same **ethnic group**. They are called ethnic Greeks. They make up about 90 percent of

Most people living in Greece are ethnic Greeks.

the population. Ethnic Greeks are very proud of their heritage. Other groups include Albanians, Aromanians, and Macedonians. These groups are quite small.

Distant Greeks

Not everyone who is an ethnic Greek lives in Greece. Many Greeks have moved to other countries. For example, in the United States, there are more than 1.3 million Greek Americans. These are people who were born in Greece or are descended from Greeks.

A flea market in Athens.

Almost two-thirds of Greeks live in cities. The cities in Greece are very modern. The rest of the population lives in rural areas. These regions are more old-fashioned. Some Greeks live on islands off the mainland.

Whether they live in a city or in the country, Greeks love their families. Often, many generations of a family live together in one home.

People in Greece use cars to get around. Mainland Greece also has a system of trains. Ferries take people to and from Greek islands.

No Car Island

On one Greek island, called Hydra, no cars are allowed. People travel by boat, on foot, or on a donkey!

In Greece, women have the same rights as men. Still, Greek women fight for equality at home and at work. This is because Greece remains a **patriarchal** society. This is especially true in rural areas.

FACT!

Greek women won the right to vote in 1952. Today, one-fifth of the members of Parliament are women.

Early Greeks worshipped many gods and goddesses. Ancient Greeks believed in twelve main gods. Zeus was the king of all gods. His wife was a goddess named Hera. Aphrodite was the goddess of love, and Ares was the

The Greek god Zeus.

god of war. Poseidon was the god of the sea.

Today, some Greeks are Muslim. Others are Jewish. However, most Greeks—about 97 percent—are Christian. They practice a type of Christianity called Eastern Orthodoxy. This type of Christianity is also called the Greek Orthodox Church.

Judaism in Greece

There used to be more Jews in Greece. However, many were killed during World War II.

Even though most Greeks are Christian, Greece has no "official" religion. Greeks are free to practice any religion they wish—or no religion at all. In fact, this right is guaranteed in the Greek constitution.

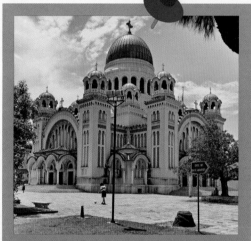

St. Andrews Cathedral in Patras, Greece, is the largest church in Greece.

The New Testament, which is part of the Christian Bible, was first written in Greek.

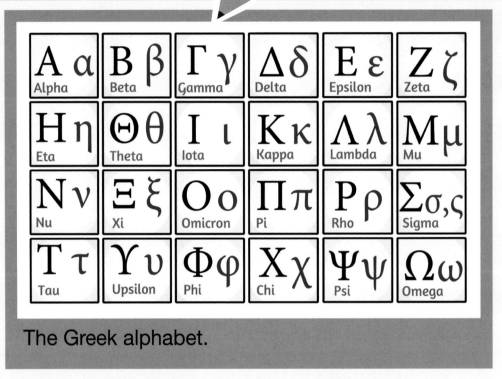

The Greek alphabet.

Greek is the official language of Greece.

Greek does not use the same letters as English (A, B, C, and so on). Instead, it uses letters in the Greek alphabet. The Greek alphabet includes letters such as Δ (delta), Π (pi), and Σ (sigma). Many of these letters are also used in mathematics.

The modern Greek language is different from the ancient Greek language. It has changed over time.

The Greek language has many versions, called **dialects**. One dialect is called the Pontic dialect. Another is the Cappadocian (cap-uh-DOE-shin) dialect.

First to Read and Write

The Greeks were one of the first people to read and write. Greeks began reading and writing in the fifteenth century BCE. They used a form of writing called Linear B. Linear B contains almost two hundred signs and symbols.

Nearly all people in Greece speak Greek. Some people also speak Turkish, Bulgarian, or Romani. Many Greeks also learn English in school.

Arts and Festivals

Greeks have enjoyed the arts since ancient times. All around Greece are beautiful buildings, sculptures, and paintings. Many of these are very old.

An ancient Greek theater.

Early Greeks were the first to write long poems, called epics, and to play music. Greeks were also the first to perform plays. These included comedies, tragedies, and histories.

Epically Famous

Two famous works of Greek literature are the *Iliad* and the *Odyssey*. Both were written by a man named Homer around 800 BCE.

Today, Greeks still enjoy plays and music. They also enjoy going to the movies, watching television, and visiting museums. The Acropolis Museum in Athens has many artifacts from ancient Greece.

Greeks celebrate several holidays. These include Greek Independence Day (March 25), Labor Day (May 1), and Ohi Day (October 28). Greeks also celebrate Christian holidays, including Christmas and Easter. Every year, Greece has many art and wine festivals.

The Greeks have played sports since ancient times. In fact, the early Greeks invented the Olympic Games. The first Olympic Games were held in 775 BCE. They continued for nearly twelve centuries. The emperor Theodosius banned them in 393 CE because they were **pagan**.

The ancient Olympics were held in honor of Zeus.

FACT!

The Olympics started as a competition between ancient Greeks. It became a worldwide competition in 1896. Greece was the first country to host these modern games.

Marathons

The running event called the marathon started in ancient Greece. A Greek messenger named Pheidippides ran from a

The Athens marathon.

town named Marathon to Athens, about 25 miles (40 kilometers) away, to announce that the Greeks had won an important battle. Today, people run marathons in honor of this event.

In ancient times, Greeks enjoyed wrestling and running. Today, they also play basketball and soccer. They call soccer football.

The Greeks also like playing games. Ancient Greeks played games like dice and board games. Many games like these are still played today.

Greek people like food. They enjoy eating vegetables, such as zucchini. They eat lots of fish, lamb, chicken, rabbit, and pork. Many meals contain a special goat cheese called feta cheese.

Moussaka

Greek cooks use lots of olive oil, lemon juice, herbs, and spices. Often, meals are served with a type of flat bread called pita bread.

One popular dish is a soup made with white beans, vegetables, and olive oil called *fasolada*. It has been eaten since ancient times.

Greek Coffee

Greeks drink a special kind of coffee. Greek coffee is boiled rather than brewed. It is very strong. Many Greeks drink three to five cups of Greek coffee every day.

Greek desserts are sweet. Many contain honey. A popular Greek dessert is called baklava. It's made with dough, butter, and nuts.

FACT!

According to tradition, Greek baklava is made with thirty-three layers of dough, one for each year of Jesus's life.

Baklava

Glossary

city-state   A city that has its own government and is its own state.

democracy   A system of government that is run by the people.

dialect   A form of a language spoken by a certain group or in a certain region.

ethnic group   A group of people who have the same cultural background.

pagan   A word that describes a religion that is not Christianity, Islam, or Judaism.

patriarchal   A word that describes a society in which men are in charge.

peninsula   A landmass that is surrounded by water on three sides.

republic   A country governed by elected people rather than by a king or queen.

Find Out More

Books

Pearson, Anne. *Ancient Greece*. DK Eyewitness Books. New York: DK Children's Press, 2014.

Peterson, Christine. *Greece*. True Books. New York: Children's Press, 2002.

Websites

History for Kids: Guide to Ancient Greece

www.historyforkids.net/ancient-greece.html

TIME for Kids Around the World: Greece

www.timeforkids.com/destination/greece

Video

The Archaeology Channel: Ancient Greece

www.archaeologychannel.org/video-guide/video-guide-menu/video-guide-summary/108-ancient-greece-pots-tell-the-story

This video talks about the history of Greece.

Index

city-state, 8–9

democracy, 11

dialect, 23

ethnic group, 16

pagan, 26

patriarchal, 19

peninsula, 6

republic, 10

About the Author

Kate Shoup has written more than thirty books and has edited hundreds more. When not working, Shoup loves to ski, read, ride her motorcycle, and watch IndyCar races. She lives in Indianapolis with her husband, her daughter, and their dog.